# A Hand B Chutneys

## Indian Chutney Recipes
### Sabita Mishra

Copyright2016

SABITA MISHRA

This book is licensed for your personal enjoyment only and may not be re-sold.

**e-mail** sabita.sbtmshr.mishra@gmail.com

## About The Book

The most interesting part of the vast Indian cuisine is the delicious chutneys and relishes; they add a different dimension to any meal and no meal is complete without them. The varieties are many and they can be prepared at home in a few minutes with easily available ingredients like tomatoes, fruits, coconut, yogurt, herbs, garlic, onion, chillies or peanuts to name a few. Home- made chutneys are healthier as they are fresh and do not contain artificial colour, flavour or preservatives. Sweet chutneys are used in breads or biscuits, the spicy ones can be used as dips and combine well with dosa/idli, upma, paratha, samosa etc. This book has mostly Indian style chutneys except for a few Asian types and guaranteed to please the taste buds.

**Table of content:**                                  **Page number**

- Apple and Date chutney                               6
- Apple –tomato chutney                                7
- Beetroot Chutney                                     8
- Channa dal Chutney(split Bengal gram)                10
- Chilli Chutney(1)                                    11
- Chilli Chutney (2)                                   12
- Coconut – mango chutney                              13
- Coconut red chilli chutney                           14
- Coconut-tomato chutney                               15
- Coconut –Yogurt chutney                              16
- Curry leave Chutney                                  18
- Curry Leaves Chutney (sweet and sour)                19
- Dry Coconut Chutney                                  20
- Date Tamarind Chutney                                21
- Date -Tomato Chutney                                 22
- Date-Pineapple chutney                               24
- Garlic carrot chutney                                25
- Garlic-coconut Chutney                               26
- Garlic chutney                                       27
- Green chilli chutney                                 28
- Green chutney with yogurt                            29
- Green Chutney with coconut                           30
- Green tomato chutney                                 31

|   | Page number |
|---|---|
| • Ginger chutney | 32 |
| • Gooseberry chutney | 34 |
| • Green mango chutney | 35 |
| • Mango-yogurt Raita | 36 |
| • Mango yogurt pachadi | 37 |
| • Mango Chutney (cooked)1 | 39 |
| • Mango Chutney (cooked) | 40 |
| • Mango-mint chutney | 41 |
| • Mint chutney sweet and sour | 42 |
| • Onion-peanut chutney | 43 |
| • Peanut chutney | 44 |
| • Plum Garlic Chutney | 45 |
| • Radish Raita | 46 |
| • Ridge gourd skin chutney | 48 |
| • Sesame Chutney | 49 |
| • Sweet Tomato chutney | 50 |
| • Tamarind-Jaggery chutney | 51 |
| • Tomato Besan( chick pea flour) Dip | 53 |
| • Tomato-Eggplant chutney | 54 |
| • Tomato onion chutney | 56 |
| • Thecha | 57 |
| • Zucchini Chutney | 58 |

# Chutney

## Apple and Date chutney

**Ingredients:**

2 cups apples chopped finely

1 cup dates chopped finely

1 cup raisins

1 cup jaggery grated

½ cup vinegar

5-6 cloves garlic

1 tsp grated ginger

1 tsp chilli powder

¼ tsp salt

½ tsp pepper powder

½ tsp lemon jest

1 tbsp lemon juice

**Method:** Cook apple, garlic and vinegar with a cup of water for 7-8 minutes till soft.

Add jaggery, dates, pepper powder, raisins and cook for another 15-20 minutes.

Add lemon jest and lemon juice and cook another 5 minutes. Transfer to a sterilized bottle and keep in the refrigerator.

### Apple –tomato chutney

**Ingredients:**

1 kg apple

1 kg tomato

¼ kg onion

4-5 cloves garlic

1 tbsp salt

1 cup sugar

2 tbsp chilli powder

2 cups vinegar

½ cup chopped dates

1 cup raisins

**Method:** Wash, peel and slice apples. Chop the tomatoes.

Boil a cup of water, add the apples and cook till soft, for about 10 minutes.

Add all other ingredients, bring to boil and reduce heat, stir to dissolve the sugar.

Cook in reduced heat for two and half hours till it is thick.

This should be stored in sterilized bottles in the refrigerator.

## Beetroot Chutney

**Ingredients:**

1 cup beet root chopped

1 onion chopped

4-5 cloves garlic

Salt to taste

1 tsp tamarind pulp

1 tbsp oil

2 broken dry red chillies

1 tbsp channa dal(split Bengal gram)

1 tsp urad dal(split black gram)

¼ tsp asafoetida

½ tsp mustard seeds

**Method:** Heat oil, add mustard seeds, when they crackle add the red chillies, asafoetida, channa dal, urad dal and fry till the dals are light brown.

Add the onion, garlic, salt and beet root and cook for 7-8 minutes till the beet root is soft.

Bring to room temperature, add tamarind and grind to make chutney.

# Channa dal Chutney (split Bengal gram)

**Ingredients:**

¼ cup roasted channa dal(split chick pea)

1 cup grated fresh coconut

Salt to taste

½ tsp grated ginger

½ cup coriander leaves

1 tbsp tamarind paste/lemon juice

3-4 cloves garlic

2-3 green chillies

1 tbsp oil

½ tsp mustard seeds

½ tsp urad dal

¼ tsp asafoetida

1 broken red chillie

**Method:** Grind chnna dal, coconut, green chillies, salt, coriander leaves, ginger, garlic to a smooth chutney by adding water.

Heat oil, add the mustard seeds, when they crackle add the urad dal, broken red chilli and asafoetida. Remove from heat and pour over the chutney.

Mix lemon juice and make the desired consistency by adding water.

### Chilli Chutney(1)

**Ingredients:**

½ cup dried red chillies, broken and seeds removed

¼ cup peeled fresh garlic

1 tsp vinegar

½ tsp soy sauce

Salt as per taste

**Method:** Pour ½ cup hot water on the chillies and allow to soak for 1 hour.

Process all the ingredients in a grinder/food processor to make a fine paste. Adjust consistency by adding ware if necessary.

This can be served with momos.

## Chilli Chutney (2)

**Ingredients:**

2 cups fresh red chillies wiped clean and chopped

½ cup green chillies wiped clean and chopped

Salt to taste

1 tbsp tamarind (not pulp)

1 tsp sugar

1 tbsp garlic chopped

½ cup mustard oil

1 tsp mustard

½ tsp nigella seeds

½ tsp fenugreek powder

4-5 broken dry red chillies

½ tsp asafoetida

**Method:** Grind the chillies, salt and tamarind and sugar to a course paste. Keep in a bottle for 2 days.

Heat oil in a pan; add the mustard seeds, nigella seeds, broken dried red chillies, asafoetida and garlic.

Pour this oil on the chilli paste, add fenugreek powder, mix.

Oil should come on top.

## Coconut – mango chutney

**Ingredients:**

½ cup fresh coconut pieces

4-5 fresh green chillies

¼ cup raw mango, skin removed and chopped

Salt to taste

1 tbsp sugar

**Method:** Grind all the ingredients to a paste.

Coconut red chilli chutney

**Ingredients:**

1 cup fresh coconut pieces

4-5 red chillies

¼ cup coriander leaves

1 tbsp roasted channa dal(split Bengal gram)

4-5 cloves garlic

Salt to taste

1 tbsp tamarind pulp

1 tsp oil

1 tsp mustard seed

A few curry leaves

1 tsp urad dal(black gram)

¼ tsp asafoetida

**Method:** Grind coconut, channa dal, salt, coriander leaves, red chillies, garlic and tamarind pulp in to a paste. Adjust consistency by adding water.

Heat oil; add mustard, when they crackle add curry leaves, urad dal and asafoetida. Pour this into the chutney.

### Coconut-tomato chutney

**Ingredients:**

1 cup chopped onion

½ cup grated fresh coconut

1 cup chopped tomato

3-4 dried red chillies

Sal to taste

1 tbsp olive oil/any oil

½ tsp cumin seeds

¼ tsp asafoetida

**Method:** Heat oil, add the cumin and red chillies, when the change colour add onion, when onion becomes transparent add the grated coconut and stir fry for 2-3 seconds. Then add the tomato and salt and cook for 2-3 minutes in medium heat till the tomatoes are soft. Bring to room temperature and grind to make chutney.

### Coconut –Yogurt chutney

**Ingredients:**

1 cup yogurt

½ cup fresh coconut pieces

2 tbsp channa dal(Bengal gram) roasted

Salt to taste

2-3 green chillies

2-3 cloves garlic

1 tsp mustard seeds

1-2 broken red chillies

¼ tsp asafoetida

1 tsp Urad(black gram dal)

1 tsp oil

**Method:** Grind channa dal, green chillies, garlic, and coconut to a paste.

Mix with the yogurt thoroughly, add salt. Adjust consistency if necessary by adding more yogurt.

Heat oil; add mustard seeds, broken red chillies, asafoetida and urad dal. When they crackle remove from heat and add ½ tsp chilli powder.

Pour this into the chutney and mix.

Serve with idli, dosa or vada

## Curry leaves Chutney

**Ingredients:**

1 cup tender curry leaves, washed

¼ cup fresh coconut

1 tbsp oil

1 tsp cumin

½ tsp mustard seeds

1 tbsp tamarind pulp

2 tbsp sugar

¼ tsp asafoetida

2 dried red chillies

Salt to taste

**Method:** Heat oil; add mustard and cumin seeds, when they crackle add red chillies and asafoetida.

Add the curry leaves and coconut, stir fry for a minute in medium heat.

Bring to room temperature, add tamarind pulp, salt and sugar and grind to a paste. Add water to adjust consistency.

## Curry Leaves Chutney (sweet and sour)

**Ingredients:**

1 cup tender curry leaves, cleaned and washed

3-4 dried red chillies

1 tbsp tamarind pulp

1 tbsp sugar or as per taste

Salt to taste

1 tbsp oil

½ tsp cumin

1 tsp mustard seeds

¼ tsp asafoetida

**Method:** Heat oil, add the mustard and cumin seeds, when they crackle add the red chillies and asafoetida along with the curry leaves and sauté for 3-4 seconds.

Remove from heat, bring to room temperature, add salt, sugar and tamarind pulp and grind to a smooth chutney.

## Dry Coconut Chutney

**Ingredients:**

1 cup fresh coconut

4-5 cloves garlic

2-3 dried red chillies

½ cup shallots

Salt to taste

1 small ball of tamarind

1 tsp oil

1 tsp urad dal(split black gram)

¼ tsp asafoetida

½ tsp mustard

**Method:** Heat oil; add the mustard, urad dal and asafoetida.

Add the coconut and stir fry for a few second without making the coconut brown.

Bring to room temperature and add the shallots and tamarind and salt.

Grind to make chutney without adding water.

### Date Tamarind Chutney

**Ingredients:**

1 cup dates, seeds removed and chopped

2 tbsp tamarind pulp

½ tsp salt

1 tsp oil

3-4 broken red chillies

1 tsp cumin

**Method:** Soak the dates in half cup water for 1 hour.

Heat oil; add the cumin and red chillies, when the chillies are crisp remove from heat. Care should be taken not to over fry them.

Add this to the soaked date and grind all other ingredients together to make chutney.

### Date -Tomato Chutney

**Ingredients:**

1 cup ripe red tomato chopped

¼ cup raisin

½ cup dates, seeds removed and chopped

Salt to taste

1 tsp oil

½ tsp mustard seeds

½ tsp fennel seeds

¼ tsp fenugreek seeds

½ tsp kalounji

¼ tsp turmeric powder

2 broken red chillies

¼ tsp asafoetida

2 tbsp sugar or as per taste

1 tbsp chopped coriander leaves

**Method:** Heat oil in a pan; add mustard, fenugreek, fennel and kalounji, when they crackle add the broken red chillies and asafoetida.

Now add the chopped tomatoes, salt, turmeric powder, cover and cook for 5 minutes.

Add the raisin and dates and cover and cook in medium heat for 6-7 minutes till the tomatoes and the dates are cooked.

Add sugar and cook 5 more minutes till the sugar melts.

Remove and add chopped coriander leaves. Serve with rice, roti or paratha.

# Date-Pineapple relish

**Ingredients:**

1 cup pine apple chopped finely

1 cup date, seeds removed and chopped finely

Salt to taste

1 tbsp oil

½ tsp mustard seeds

¼ tsp asafoetida

½ tsp kalounji

½ tsp fennel seeds

1 tbsp tamarind pulp

1 tbsp jaggery

½ tsp turmeric powder

½ tsp chilli powder

**Method:** Heat oil; add mustard, fennel, and kalounji, when they crackle add the asafoetida, chopped pine apple and dates. Add salt, turmeric powder, chilli powder and cover and cook in medium heat till the dates are soft.

Add the tamarind pulp and jaggery and cover and cook again in low heat till the jaggery has melted.

### Garlic carrot chutney

**Ingredients:**

1 cup carrot chopped

5-6 cloves garlic

Salt to taste

1 tbsp coriander leaves

2-3 green chillies

1 tbsp lemon juice

1 tsp vinegar

½ tsp cumin

½ tsp mustard seeds

1 tsp olive oil/any oil

**Method:** Heat oil in a pan and add the mustard and cumin seeds and red chillies.

Remove from heat when done. Add all other ingredients and grind to a coarse paste.

### Garlic-coconut Chutney

**Ingredients:**

8-10 cloves garlic

1 tbsp oil

2-3 whole dried red chillies

1 cup grated coconut

1 tbsp tamarind pulp

Salt to taste

1 tsp mustard seeds

½ tsp cumin

½ tsp sugar

**Method:** Heat oil in a pan; add the mustard seeds and cumin, when they crackle add the chillies and garlic. Stir continuously.

Add the coconut and sauté for a minute in medium heat. Bring to room temperature.

Add tamarind pulp and grind to a paste.

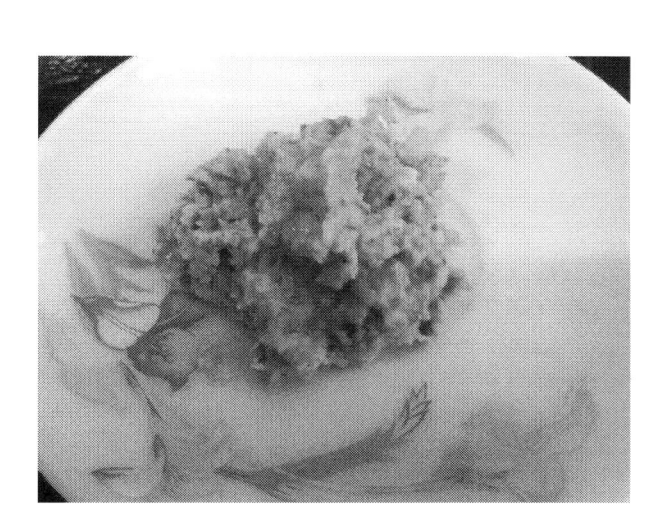

### Garlic chutney

**Ingredients:**

½ cup garlic peeled

3-4 green chillies

Salt to taste

1 tbsp lemon juice

1 tbsp olive oil/mustard oil

**Method**: Heat oil, add the garlic and the green chillies and fry for 3-4 minutes in medium heat till they are soft.

Bring to room temperature and grind to a paste with salt and lemon juice.

## Green chilli chutney

**Ingredients**:

10 green chillies

A small ball of tamarind

Salt to taste

2-3 cloves garlic

1 tbsp oil

1 tsp sugar

**Method:** Heat oil, add the green chillies and garlic and stir fry for a minute till the chillies are soft.

Bring to room temperature, add salt, tamarind and grind to make chutney.

## Green chutney with yogurt

**Ingredients:**

1 cup coriander leaves

½ cup mint leaves

Salt to taste

1 tsp grated ginger

3-4 cloves garlic

2-3 green chillies

½ tsp lemon juice

1 cup yogurt

**Method:** Grind all the ingredients except yogurt to a paste, mix with beaten yogurt, adjust consistency by adding more yogurt if necessary

This chutney can be used as a dip also.

### Green Chutney with coconut

**Ingredients:**

1 cup chopped coriander leaves

½ cup mint leaves

1 tbsp lemon juice

Salt to taste

3-4 green chillies

3-4 cloves garlic

¼ cup fresh grated coconut

**Method:** Grind all the ingredients to make smooth chutney, add water to adjust consistency.

### Green tomato chutney

**Ingredients:**

1 cup green tomato chopped

1 cooking apple chopped

1 cup dates chopped

¼ cup garlic chopped

¼ cup raisins

½ cup sugar

1 cup vinegar

½ tsp salt

1 tbsp chilli powder

½ tsp cardamom powder

½ tsp cinnamon powder

½ tsp pepper powder

**Method:** Cook tomato, apple, and dates for about 12-minutes in medium heat till soft.

Add the raisins, salt, sugar, vinegar, cardamom powder, pepper powder, chilli powder, cinnamon powder and cook again for about 20 minutes in low heat, stirring at regular intervals so that it does not stick to the bottom.

Keep in the fridge in sterilized jars.

## Ginger chutney

**Ingredients:**

2 tbsp ginger chopped

4-5 cloves garlic

2 tbsp onion chopped

Salt to taste

2 dry red chillies

1 tbsp oil

1 tsp tamarind pulp

½ tsp cumin

½ tsp sugar

**Method:** Heat oil, add cumin seeds and red chillies, when they are done add garlic, onion and ginger.

Fry till the onion changes colour but not brown.

Remove from heat, add salt and tamarind, sugar and grind to a paste.

# Gooseberry chutney

**Ingredients:**

1 cup chopped gooseberry seeds removed

Salt to taste

1 tsp mustard

5-6 green chillies

½ tsp turmeric powder

1 tsp red chilli powder

½ tsp asafoetida

2 tbsp mustard oil/ any oil

**Method:** Boil a cup of water, add the chopped gooseberries in to it and cook for 7-10 minutes. Bring to room temperature.

Grind the gooseberries and green chillies to a course paste.

Heat oil in a pan, add the mustard seeds, when they are done add the paste, salt, turmeric powder, asafoetida and red chilli powder and cook in medium heat for 4-5 minutes.

## Green mango chutney

**Ingredients:**

½ cup green mango, peeled and chopped

Salt to taste

2-3 cloves garlic

3-4 green chillies

1 tbsp sugar or depending on the sourness of the mango

**Method:** Grind all the ingredients to make chutney.

## Mango-yogurt Raita

**Ingredients**:

1 cup hung curd

¾ cup ripe mango pulp

Salt to taste

½ tsp black pepper powder

½ tsp chilli powder

½ cup fresh mint leaves finely chopped

1 tsp honey

**Method:** Hung curd is prepared by removing water from the normal yogurt. Tie the yogurt in a muslin cloth and keep hanging for a few hours till all the water drains out.

Process all ingredients except mint leaves in a mixer/food processor to mix them thoroughly.

Add mint leaves and mix.

Serve with puri or paratha or use as a dip.

## Mango yogurt pachadi

**Ingredients:**

1 cup hung curd

¾ cup green mango peeled and grated

Salt to taste

1 tsp sugar or as required depending on the sourness of the mango

2-3 chopped green chillies

¼ tsp ginger grated

1 tbsp garlic chopped

1 tbsp coriander leaves chopped

1 tsp fresh mint leaves chopped

1 tsp mustard seeds

¼ tsp asafoetida

A few curry leaves

1 tsp split urad(split black gram)

1-2 broken red chillies

1 tbsp oil

**Method:** Process the hung curd in a mixer/food processor to make it smooth.

Heat oil in a pan; add mustard seeds, when they crackle add the red chillies, urad dal and asafoetida and the curry leaves stir fry for 1-2 seconds.

Add garlic and green chillies, when they change colour add the grated mango, salt and sugar.

Cook in medium heat till the mango is cooked.

Bring to room temperature and mix with the processed hung curd.

Mix thoroughly and add mint and coriander leaves.

Heat a tbsp of oil in a pan, add mustard seeds and broken red chillies, when they crackle remove from heat and add ½ tsp of chilli powder, pour this over the pachadi; this adds colour. This is optional.

This can be served as a dip also.

# Mango Chutney (cooked)1

**Ingredients:**

1 cup fresh green mango, peeled and cut in to pieces

1 cup sugar

½ tsp salt

½ tsp crushed ginger

½ tsp crushed garlic

1 tsp chilli powder

2-3 cloves

2 green cardamoms

1 inch piece cinnamon

½ cup vinegar

**Method:** Add salt, sugar, cardamom, cloves, cinnamon, chilli, turmeric to the mango pieces and mix thoroughly. Keep covered for 6-7 hours.

Cook in medium temperature till it thickens for 20-25 minutes. Add vinegar, bring to boil and remove from heat.

This should be stored in sterilized bottles when cool.

### Mango Chutney (cooked)2

**Ingredients:**
2 cups raw mango without stone cut in to pieces
A pinch salt
1 tsp chilli powder
½ tsp turmeric powder

1 tbsp oil

½ tsp nigella seeds

½ tsp fennel seeds

¼ tsp asafoetida

1 cup jaggery or sugar (or as per taste)

**Method:** Heat oil in a pan, add fennel seeds and nigella seeds, when they are done add asafoetida, the mango pieces, salt, turmeric powder and chilli powder.

Mix, cover and cook in low temperature for 10 minutes stirring once in a while till the mangoes are soft.

Add sugar/jaggery; cover and cook again in low heat for 10 minutes till the sugar has melted.

Cook open for 2-3 minutes till it is slightly thick.

Store in sterilized bottles and keep in the fridge.

## Mango-mint chutney

**Ingredients:**

1 cup green mango chopped

½ cup mint

¼ cup grated coconut

Salt to taste

2-3 green chillies

2-3 cloves garlic

1 tbsp sugar

**Method:** Grind all the ingredients to make a smooth chutney, adjust consistency by adding water.

This can be used as a dip also.

**Mint chutney sweet and sour**

**Ingredients:**

1 cup fresh mint leaves cleaned

3-4 fresh green chillies

Salt to taste

1 tbsp tamarind pulp

1 tbsp sugar or as per taste

**Method:** Grind all the ingredients to make a smooth chutney.

## Onion-peanut chutney

**Ingredients:**

1 big onion sliced

2 tbsp peanut, roasted with little oil

2 dry red chillies

2-3 cloves garlic

1 tbsp oil

A small ball of tamarind

Salt to taste

**Method:** Heat oil, add the sliced onion and fry till it changes colour. Add the red chillies, garlic and the roasted peanuts, fry for 10 seconds.

Bring to room temperature, add salt and tamarind and grind to a paste, add water to adjust consistency.

## Peanut chutney

**Ingredients:**

½ cup roasted pea nut

½ cup fresh grated coconut

Salt to taste

1 tbsp lemon juice

3-4 fresh green chillies

½ cup coriander leaves

2-3 cloves garlic

½ tsp grated ginger

1 tsp roasted sesame (Til)

**Method:** Grind all the ingredients except lemon juice to a paste, add lemon juice and mix. Adjust consistency by adding water as per requirement.

## Plum Garlic Chutney

**Ingredients:**

2 green apples chopped

½ kg plum, seeds removed

2 cups sugar

A pinch salt

1 onion chopped

10-12 cloves garlic chopped

2 cups apple cider vinegar

2-3 star anise

½ tsp cinnamon powder

**Method:** Place all ingredients except plum in a big pot and bring to boil. Reduce heat, cover and cook for 20-30 minutes till the apples are soft.

Add the plums and cook for another 30 minutes

Keep in the fridge in sterilized bottles.

**Radish Raita**

**Ingredients:**

1 cup grated radish

1 cup yogurt

Salt to taste

1 tsp oil

½ tsp mustard seeds

¼ tsp asafoetida

A few curry leaves

1 tbsp chopped coriander

1 red chilli broken

½ tsp urad dal(split black gram)

**Method**: Mix yogurt and grated radish.

Heat oil, add mustard seeds, when they crackle add curry leaves, urad dal, asafoetida, broken red chilli, when the aroma stars coming remove from heat and pour over the radish-yogurt mixture. Sprinkle the chopped coriander.

# Ridge gourd skin chutney

**Ingredients:**

1 cup thick ridge gourd skin

1 tbsp tamarind pulp

1 small onion

2-3 cloves garlic

Salt to taste

2 tbsp sugar

1 tbsp olive oil/any oil

½ tsp cumin

1 tsp mustard

2-3 red chillies

**Method:** Heat oil in frying pan, add the mustard and cumin seeds, when they crackle add the red chillies.

Add onion and garlic; when they are light brown add the ridge gourd skin and salt.

Cover and cook for 3-4 minutes in medium heat stirring once in a while till the skin is soft.

Bring to room temperature, add the tamarind pulp, sugar and grind to a paste.

## Sesame Chutney

**Ingredients:**

½ cup sesame roasted

2 tbsp coriander leaves

2-3 cloves garlic

Salt to taste

1 tbsp lemon juice

½ tsp sugar

1 tbsp fresh grated coconut

**Method**: Dry roast the sesame seeds and bring to room temperature.

Grind all the ingredients to a paste, add water to adjust consistency.

**Sweet Tomato chutney**

**Ingredients:**

1 kg tomato, washed and chopped

½ kg onion chopped

6-7 cloves garlic

4 fresh red chillies chopped

1 tbsp chilli powder

¼ kg jaggery

1 cup vinegar

½ tsp cardamom powder

½ tsp grated ginger

1 tsp salt

**Method:** Bring all the ingredients to boil, reduce heat and cook for 7-8 minutes till they are soft. Bring to room temperature and process to make chutney. Adjust consistency as per taste.

Store the chutney in a sterilized bottle in the refrigerator.

**Tamarind-Jaggery chutney**

**Ingredients:**

½ cup thick tamarind pulp

¼ cup grated crushed jaggery or as per taste

¼ tsp salt

½ tsp black pepper powder

¼ tsp turmeric powder

½ tsp chilli powder

½ tsp roasted cumin powder

**Method:** Add jaggery, salt, turmeric powder, chilli powder to the tamarind pulp and bring to boil, reduce temperature and cook for 7-10 minutes till the jaggery is dissolved. Add pepper powder and cumin powder and cook for 2-3 minutes more.

Adjust consistency as per requirement.

Bring to room temperature and store in a dry glass jar in the fridge.

This can be used with samosa, dhokla etc.

# Tomato Besan( chick pea flour) Dip

**Ingredients:**

1 cup tomato chopped

1 tbsp chick pea flour

Salt to taste

1 tbsp chopped onion

1 tsp chopped garlic

1 tbsp oil

½ tsp mustard seeds

2 broken red chillies

¼ tsp asafoetida

½ tsp sugar

1 tsp chopped coriander leaves

**Method**: Heat oil; add mustard seeds, broken red chillies, when they crackle add asafoetida, onion and garlic. When they change colour add the tomato puree, salt, sugar and allow to cook for 2-3 minutes in medium heat.

Add chick pea flour to half cup of water mix properly without keeping lumps, add this to the tomato and cook for 3-4 minutes more. Adjust consistency by adding water if necessary. Remove when the mixture thickens slightly. Serve with chopped coriander leaves

This can be used as a dip.

## Tomato-Eggplant chutney

**Ingredients:**

1 cup tomato chopped

½ cup eggplant chopped

1 onion chopped

2-3 cloves garlic

2-3 green chillies

1-2 dries red chillies

1 tbsp oil

1 tsp cumin seeds

¼ tsp asafoetida

Salt to taste

½ cup coriander leaves

1 tbsp tamarind pulp

1 tsp sugar

**Method:** heat oil in a thick pan; add the cumin seeds and red chillies, when the cumin is brown add the onion, garlic, green chillies and asafoetida.

When the onion is transparent add the eggplant and tomatoes, salt. Cover and cook in medium heat for 4-5 minutes, stirring once in a while till they are soft.

Remove from heat, bring to room temperature, add the tamarind pulp and sugar and grind to make chutney

# Tomato onion chutney

**Ingredients:**

1 big onion chopped

3-4 cloves garlic chopped

1 cup tomato chopped

Salt to taste

1 tbsp tamarind pulp

1 tbsp oil

1 tsp mustard seeds

3-4 broken red chillies

1 tsp urad dal (black gram)

¼ tsp asafoetida

**Method:** Heat oil in a pan, when hot, the red chillies, onion and garlic and cook till they are soft but not brown.

Add the tomatoes, salt, asafoetida and cook till the tomatoes are soft.

Remove from heat, bring to room temperature, add tamarind pulp and grind to a smooth paste.

Heat 1 tsp oil, add the mustard seed, when done add the curry leaves and urad dal.

When the urad dal is light brown pour this on the chutney and mix.

## Thecha

**Ingredients:**

10-12 green chillies

½ cup coriander leaves

¼ cup garlic

Salt to taste

1 tbsp lemon juice/ raw mango if available

1 tsp oil

**Method**: Heat oil in a pan, add garlic and green chillies. When they are soft add the coriander leaves and sauté for 10 seconds.

Remove from heat; bring to room temperature.

Add salt and lemon juice/raw mango and hand pound coarsely.

## Zucchini Chutney

**Ingredients:**

1 cup zucchini chopped

1 tbsp roasted peanut

- 3-4 cloves garlic
- 1 tbsp tamarind pulp/lemon juice
- ½ cup coriander leaves
- ¼ cup fresh mint
- Salt to taste
- 2-3 green chillies
- ½ cup fresh coconut pieces
- ¼ tsp asafoetida
- 1 tbsp oil
- 1 tsp mustard seeds
- ½ tsp cumin
- 2 broken red chillies
- 1 tsp black gram (urad dal)

**Method**: Heat oil, add mustard seeds, when they crackle add cumin, red chillies, urad dal, asafoetida, and garlic. Stir fry for a few seconds.

Add the zucchini, salt, green chillies and coconut and cook covered till the zucchini is soft.

Remove from heat and bring to room temperature.

Add roasted peanut, coriander leaves and mint to this mixture and grind to a paste. Adjust consistency by adding water.

**Note: Vegetables like ridge gourd, bottle gourd, onion and cabbage can be made chutney in the same process.**

Printed in Great Britain
by Amazon